THE SALT WE BLEED

THE SALT WE BLEED

DENILE BAUGH

BELLE ISLE BOOKS
www.belleislebooks.com

ISBN (Paperback): 978-1-966369-57-8
Library of Congress Control Number: 2025926225

Designed by Sami Langston
Project managed by Sydney Wright

Published by
Belle Isle Books (an imprint of Brandylane Publishers, Inc.)
5 S. 1st Street
Richmond, Virginia 23219

BELLE ISLE BOOKS
www.belleislebooks.com

belleislebooks.com | brandylanepublishers.com

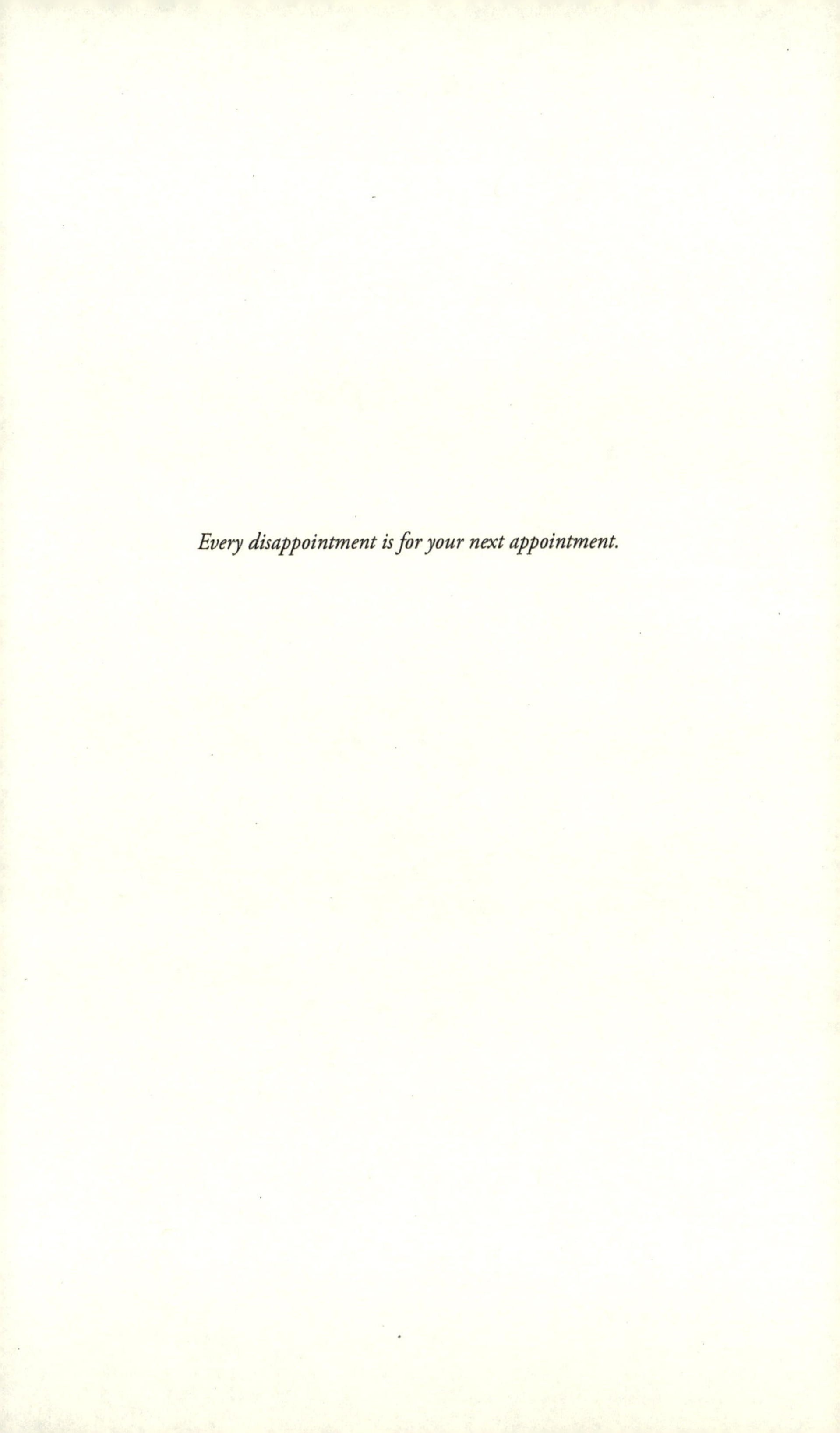

Every disappointment is for your next appointment.

Contents

Introduction

The Salt We Bleed is not merely a collection of poems; it is a collection born from the raw and often painful process of living, of loving, and of facing the truth that we are all, in one way or another, both beautiful and broken. It is an exploration of the heart's most intimate journey, and a reflection of the ways we ache, heal, and ultimately, rediscover ourselves.

The poems in this collection are born from moments of intense introspection and raw emotion. They are the echoes of moments that linger long after they've passed, the traces of emotions that refuse to fade, and the memories that return to us like waves, carrying with them the salt of our tears, the warmth of our joy, and ultimately find a path to healing.

This collection invites you to step into the most vulnerable parts of yourself, to journey through the light and the darkness that dwells within us all. It is a map of the heart, tracing the contours of love's beginnings, the fissures of heartbreak, and the quiet, sacred work of healing that follows. Each poem is a step along this path, a reflection of the different ways we encounter, endure, and ultimately rise from the trials of being human.

In **The Blossoming**, we are reminded of the magic that exists in the first stirrings of love—the way it blooms suddenly, fiercely, like wildflowers in an untamed field. It is a chapter of hope and wonder, where every heartbeat feels like a melody and every word exchanged is a promise wrapped in light.

In **The Unraveling,** we encounter the shadows that creep into even the brightest of places, the doubts and fears that tug at the threads of connection. Here, we face the discomfort of seeing love slip away, of recognizing that what once felt eternal can become fragile, delicate, and fleeting.

The Fallout confronts us with the aftermath of love's destruction—the sharp edges of grief, the silence left behind when words no longer bridge the distance between two souls. It is a place of reckoning, where we are forced to confront our own pain, to sit with the emptiness that follows when love is torn away. These poems do not shy away from the ache; they embrace it, allowing us to feel every cut, every wound, with an honesty that is both brutal and liberating.

In **The Reflection**, we turn inward, searching for the pieces of ourselves that remain, seeking to understand, to heal, and to grow. It is a journey of self-discovery, a quiet acceptance of who we are beyond the labels of 'broken' or 'whole.' These poems speak to the resilience that lies within us, the courage to rise from the ashes and begin again, to find beauty, not despite the scars but because of them.

The Salt We Bleed is an invitation—to feel, to remember, and to embrace the messy, chaotic, and profoundly beautiful experience of being alive. It is a testament to the power of love, in all its forms, to shape us, to shatter us, and to rebuild us into something stronger, something truer. As you turn these pages, may you find pieces of your own story within the lines, and may you discover that you are never alone in your journey. This is the salt we bleed, the truth that binds us, and the love that carries us home.

Section I: The Blossoming

There's a sweetness here, a dizzying dance of glances and stolen moments that linger like honey on the tongue. This is the season of blooming, where petals unfurl and hearts beat in wild, reckless rhythm, where every word feels like magic whispered into the dark.

Chance Romance

There was no one else
That made sense.
We met by pure circumstance,
But I just knew,
When I met you,
All my life had been suspense.

In the moment that I met your eyes

I realized
That you were all I'd fantasized.
Every dream,
It seemed, was fulfilled.
In that moment, time stood still.

I didn't understand,
But you took my hand,
And your smile sent shivers across my skin.
Now I'm trapped
And wrapped up tight,
Around your moon like a satellite.

With each word you spoke,
New perspectives
And ideologies
Awoke in me.
With new insight, I'll overwrite,

The past that was once shrouded in night.

You brought me light
To see with clarity.
I fell for you with intensity,
In reverie,
A new discovery
Of newfound authenticity.

Guiding me slow, complete incognito,

We defied the status quo,
With the bond we share,
This brief affair,
Unseen, deceit,
Two hearts, one beat,
Inhibitions obsolete.

There was no one else,
That made sense.
We met by pure circumstance,
But in this dance,
This chance romance,
You changed my world in an instant.

Let's Drink

Join me for a drink,
Let's sip, talk, and think.
Take me to the brink
Of all the things you've seen and done.
Come, my friend, and share with me
This evanescent dance of memory,
Where past and present both agree
To paint the night until it's won.

Raise your glass and let us toast,
To moments cherished, time engrossed,
In whispered words and secrets close,
We'll journey till the rising sun.

Through laughter's light and shadows steep,
In conversations vast and deep,
Together, promises we'll keep
In the silence where our thoughts are spun.

Speak of journeys far and near,
Of triumphs grand and subtle fear.
In your words, the stars appear,
Their light reflects how far we've come.

We'll trace the lines of fate's design
In silvered threads of times refine.
With every drop of vintage wine,
A tale untold, a song divine.

Join me for a drink,
Let's sip, and talk, and think.
Take me to the brink
Of all the things you've seen and done.
Come, my friend, and share with me,

This evanescent dance of memory,
Where past and present both agree
To paint the night until it's won.

We'll walk through gardens of the mind,
Where every leaf and bloom remind
Me of moments left in time confined,
Yet in our hearts forever kind.

With every clink of glass, a bridge,
From now to then, from ridge to ridge,
We cross the gaps that time abridge,
And find ourselves in sweet liaison.

Through the depths of night, we'll roam,
In stories that become our home,
In every whispered word and poem,
We'll find the dawn of new begun.

In crystal clarity, our dreams align
In reflections pure and memories fine.
Together, let our hearts entwine
In moments where our souls are one.

Join me for a drink,
Let's sip and talk and think.
Take me to the brink
Of all the things you've seen and done
Come, my friend, and share with me
This evanescent dance of memory,
Where past and present both agree
To paint the night until it's won.

Conversation Casanova

There's magic in the way he speaks.
In his words, I find the joy I seek.
He's got me, there's no turning back—
I'm falling fast on this one-way track.

My conversation Casanova,
Wrap me in your sweet aroma.
Your voice, like sweetened velvet wine,
Captivates me, line by line.

Every syllable and gentle phrase
Leads me deep into your gaze.
You've got me, I'm falling over—
My conversation Casanova.

Eyes that hold a thousand tales,
Lips that tip the balanced scales.
You've won me; I'm surrendering,
To the serenade you're rendering.

You speak of things I've never heard,
I hang onto your every word.
No written line could ever compare
To the way you hold me with your stare.

In the spaces between, we find salvation—
In the language of our own creation.
Every word, a revelation—
In love with our conversations.

There's danger in this game we play,
But I'm willing, so come what may.
Every sentence gives me a reason
To stay with you through every season.

I'm lost, completely, willingly,
In this movement of words, thrilling me.
The power you hold, unknowingly,
Is the warmth that hugs me lovingly.

It's more than just chemistry—
It's mental synergy.
Your thoughts are endless galaxies,
Unlocking doors with subtlety.

I trace the path where laughter walks,
In the echo of our late-night talks.
It's not your touch that pulls me close,
But your stories that make my heart overdose.

To some, you may seem unusual,
But with you, it feels so natural.
Your inner thoughts are so lyrical,
Inching closer to the physical.

There's no escape; I'm bound by choice,
To the melody of your wicked voice.
Intoxicated by your articulate tongue,
I've fallen deeply for this dialogue Don Juan.

Unsupervised

I apologize,
In my defense, I was left unsupervised.
The moon was full, and I felt alive,
I couldn't resist this urge inside.

Soft touches, melting with such ease,
A dance of lovers, begging to please.
The night was hot, a thrilling breeze,
Whispers of passion between my knees.

Eyes met, ignited bright,
Lips brushed, a pure delight.
Bodies tangled, lost in night,
Surrendered to the lunar light.

Hands roamed freely, fingers traced,
Every curve and hidden place,
Garments abandoned in fevered haste,
No inch of skin was left uncased.

Breathless voices, heated moans,
Flesh on flesh, and aching groans,
Together in this primal zone,
Two bodies, one desire alone.

Sweat glistened, skin on fire,
Every touch a sharp desire,
Movements matched, climbing higher,
Lost in waves of sweet transpire.
Beneath the sheets, we intertwine,
Rhythmic thrusts and gasps combined,
In this moment, souls aligned,
A world of pleasure, undefined.

Nails raked gently down a spine,
Shivers sparked, sensual signs,
Teeth marks along the neckline,
Inhibitions left behind.

Hips pressed closer, movements slow,
Building heat in every throw,
A secret language, ebb and flow,
We divide the skies and give the stars a show.

Hands gripped tight, pulling hair
With every sigh, scream, and cheer,
Passion's path became so clear,
Each touch a spark, each kiss sincere.

Mangled hair and mingled scents,
An orchestra of sweet fragrance,
Desires found in dark decadence
Lost in the night's sinful events.

With every arch and every grind,
Ecstasy of hearts combined,
A moment lost, no longer blind,
At pleasure's peak, we both unwind.

Morning comes, a soft reprise,
Lovers parted with tender sighs,
A moment shared in each other's eyes,
Of moonlit nights and wild cries.

Messy Dress

She's a mess in a cocktail dress,
A blend of chaos and finesse,
A temptress cloaked in innocence,
Alluring in silhouette.

Her touch, a ghostly soft caress,
Her laughter, like a sparkling wine,
A fleeting trace of tenderness,
Intoxicating and divine.

Her eyes hold the universe,
With secrets to unfold,
A swirling storm of passion,
fierce and uncontrolled.

She wears her scars like jewelry,
Each one a testament,
To battles fought and won,
In a life of discontent.

She walks a path of contradictions,
Where day and night collide,
A nomad of emotions,
with no place left to hide.

She's the chaos in the calm,
The calm within the storm,
A living metaphor,
In a most enchanting form.

She's a symphony of chaos,
A melody of grace,
A complex composition,
In a simple, stunning space.

Her hair, a wild cascade
That refuses to be tamed,
A statement to her freedom
In a world that's so constrained.

She's a mess in a cocktail dress,
Yet perfect in her flaws,
A beautiful confusion,
Breaking all the laws.

Serpent Eyes

Diamond hips and velvet smile,
Leaves you haunted, mesmerized,
She lures you in with serpent eyes,
You'll lose yourself to her sweet disguise.

She weaves a web of dark delight,
Ensnaring hearts within the night,
Her gaze intense, her laughter light,
Her kiss, a mark, her love, a bite.

For those who fall beneath her gaze,
Are left to wander in a daze.
Her beauty's trap, a tangled maze,
Where dreams are lost in passion's blaze.

Moonlit skin and silky sighs,
A siren's call that never dies,
In her embrace, your spirit flies,
But morning brings harsh goodbyes.

A phantom touch that lingers still,
A void that nothing else can fill,
She holds your heart against your will,
A passion that can break or kill.

Diamond hips and velvet smile,
Leaves you haunted, mesmerized,
She lures you in with serpent eyes,
You'll lose yourself to her sweet disguise.

Her beauty is a deadly game,
A burning fire, a raging flame,
Once you're caught, you're never the same,
A victim of her love's claim.

She moves with grace, a silent threat,
A dangerous path, a risky bet,
In shadows where her secrets set,
A love that's hard to forget.

With every step, she binds you tight,
A dance that lasts throughout the night,
Her touch, a mix of wrong and right,
Her world, a haven out of sight.

Diamond hips and velvet smile,
Leaves you haunted, mesmerized,
She lures you in with serpent eyes,
You'll lose yourself to her sweet disguise.

So, heed the warning if you dare,
Those serpent eyes, a danger rare,
A love that tempts but brings despair,
A figure in the twilight air.

A fleeting star in night's embrace,
A haunting look, a hidden face,
Her love, a fire that leaves no trace,
Yet memories time can't erase.

Diamond hips and velvet smile,
Leave you longing, paralyzed,
Her serpent eyes that tantalize,
You'll lose yourself to her sweet disguise.

Can I?

I can feel the weight you bear,
The muted screams, that vacant stare,
A soul burdened beyond compare.
I can feel the weight you bear.

I can see the storm you hold inside,
Facing terrors you can't confide,
Seeking the peace you've been denied,
I can see the storm you hold inside.
I can sense the nights alone,
Haunted by the things you've known,
Endless hours, chilled to the bone,
I can sense the nights alone.

I can hear echoes of your wasted years,
I can listen to your whispered fears.
Drowning in seas of your own tears.
I can hear echoes of your wasted years.

I can see your heart's deep ache,
Every tremor, every quake,
Every smile you must fake,
I can see your heart's deep ache.

I can touch the scars you hide,
The battles fought and tears you've dried,
The silent cries where dreams have died,
I can touch the scars you hide.

I can feel your heavy heart,
Worn and torn and ripped apart,
Searching for a brand-new start,
I can feel your heavy heart.

Can I share the path you tread?
Every tear and word unsaid,
In the journey where you've bled,
Can I share the path you tread?

Do You

Do you still think of me,
When I'm far away,
Although we haven't spoken,
For years, months, and days?

Do the songs we cherished still play,
Deep inside your mind,
In the symphony of life
Where our hearts were aligned?

Does the touch of nostalgia,
Bring a gentle smile
As you travel alone
Down memory's mile?

Though distance and time,
Have drawn us apart,
Do I still linger somewhere
Deep inside your heart?

Do the scents of the season,
Bring back the days,
When we walked side by side,
Through life's intricate maze?

Does a breeze carry whispers,
Of our times gone by
As you gaze at the stars,
In the midnight sky?

Do you still think of me,
When I'm far away,
Although we haven't spoken,
For years, months, and days?

Do you recall the laughter,
The dreams we shared,
The times when we felt
That the world truly cared?

Do you hear my voice,
In the whispering breeze,
In the rustle of leaves,
In the sigh of the trees?

Do you wonder where I am,
What paths I've crossed,
In the mosaic of life,
In the moments we've lost?

Do you think of me,
When I'm out of sight,
When the day fades,
Gently into night?

So, if you find yourself
In a thoughtful state,
Know that I too,
Often contemplate.

If you still think of me,
When I'm far away,
Although we haven't spoken,
For years, months, and days?

Though we've drifted apart,
And our lives rearranged,
Does a part of you feel
That some things haven't changed?

Section II: The Unraveling

There is a silence that follows love—a space where shadows gather, and truth slips through the cracks. What was once whole begins to fray, thread by trembling thread, and we find ourselves tangled in the questions we never dared to ask.

Call and Response

I called you,
But you ignored me.
Your silence,
It implored me
To question
Your intentions,
And the love,
That you swore me.

You pretended
That you need me,
Then act like
You don't see me.
Your coldness
deceived me,
And left me feeling,
Alone and empty.

You promised,
You adored me,
Then vanished,
And ignored me.
Now I see
What you showed me
Was never love,
It was just a story.

I cried out,
But you denied me.
Your absence
Amplified me
In the echoes
Of our memories,
Where your ghost
Still defies me.

You built walls
To confine me
With your lies
That blind me.
Now the truth,
Has unchained me
From the hurt
That enslaves me.

I walked away,
And you just let me,
But your indifference
Has set me,
Free from chains,
That beset me
From a love
That will forget me.

Overthinking

I'm thinking about him again,
It's coming back and torturing
Me with thoughts of what could have been,
Why do I keep thinking of him?

I see his face so very clear,
He's everywhere and it's not fair.
He left me here so unprepared,
With nothing but these dried-up tears.

His voice echoes in my mind,
A reminder that I was left behind.
It's haunting me, with chill down my spine,
Leaving me bitter and resigned.

I see his smile in crowded places,
His laugh in unfamiliar faces,
A past that never truly faded,
A love that left me feeling jaded.

I'm thinking about him again,
It's coming back and torturing
Me with thoughts of what could have been,
Why do I keep thinking of him?

Why does my heart betray my will,
A wounded love that haunts me still?
What-ifs and could-have-beens,
Are chains that bind me from within.
The world spins on, yet here I stay,
In reveries of yesterday.
These memories haunt me every day,
Reminding me that he didn't stay.

Why does my heart defy my plea,
To let him go, to set me free
From love that wasn't meant to be,
An unrequited fantasy.

I'm thinking about him again,
It's coming back and torturing
Me with thoughts of what could have been,
Why do I keep thinking of him?

Wanting

I wanted to say so much,
But said so little,
Felt so much,
But still, I didn't
Speak a word
When I had the chance.
Now you've moved,
Out of my glance.

I wanted to hate you,
But I couldn't,
It was too hard.
My heart wouldn't
Let me move on,
It was too rough.
I hate myself,
Cause I wasn't enough.

I wanted to cry,
But tears wouldn't fall,
Held it inside,
And built up a wall.
Wanted to scream,
But no sound came out;
Wanted to run,
But stood still in doubt.

I wanted to give you my all,
But was left with none.
Wanted to fight battles,
But the war wasn't won.
Wanted to chase dreams,
But was caught in a trance;
I wanted to dance,
But missed the chance.

I wanted to forget you,
But memories lingered;
Your touch, your voice,
Your words, your fingers.
A shadow that follows,
A ghost in my mind,
No matter how far,
You're always close behind.

I wanted a remedy,
But wounds stay open;
Time moves forward,
Yet I'm still frozen.
Life has a way
Of closing doors,
Leaving us stranded
On separate shores.

I wanted to grow,
But felt too small;
Wanted to stand tall,
But continued to fall.
Wanted to believe,
But my faith was shattered;
I wanted to repair,
But nothing mattered.

I wanted to heal,
But the pain's too deep;
Wanted to dream,
But I can't even sleep.
Wanted to find peace,
But it eludes me still,
I wanted to get pass this,
But I don't think I will.

Why

Why didn't you fight for me, the way I fought for you?
I would have given you the stars, the sun, and moon.

Why did you let me go, when I held on so tight?
I would've faced the darkest days, to bring you the light.

Why didn't you stand by me, as I stood by your side?
I would've crossed the wildest seas, against the roughest tide.

Why'd you leave me here, with dreams we could've shared?
I would've braved the fiercest storms, if only you cared.

Why didn't you see my love, the way I saw yours true?
I would've built a world for us, only me and you.

Why didn't you fight for me, the way I fought for you?
I would've given you the stars, the sun, and moon.

Why did you let me fall, when I was there to catch your fears?
I would've wiped away your pain and dried all your tears.

Why did you break my heart, when I gave you my trust?
I would've followed you through life, as love demands we must.

Why did you shut me out, when I opened every door?
I would've walked a thousand miles, to give you even more.

Why did you shatter hopes, when I built them so high?
I would've flown on broken wings, just to reach your sky.

Why didn't you fight for me, the way I fought for you?
I would've given you the stars, the sun, and moon.

Why didn't you believe in us, as I believed in fate?
I would've waited endlessly, despite how long it takes.

Why didn't you hear my cries, the way I heard your pleas?
I would've bent the universe to set your mind at ease.

Why didn't you lift me up, as I rose to your defense?
I would've fought a thousand battles, if you'd given me a chance.

Why didn't you fight for me, the way I fought for you?
I would've given you the stars, the sun, and moon too.

Someone New

I see you now with someone new,
Doing the things we used to do,
Does she know what you have planned?
Is she just another grain of sand?

She laughs like I used to,
Thinking that your love is true.
But little does she know the game
That leaves no heart without a stain.

Does she know she'll be left behind,
When you change your heart like you change your mind?
You paint the skies, but the colors fade,
Leaving her lost in the mess you've made.

Does she know what's hiding there?
Behind those eyes, beneath that stare?
She sees a future in your smile,
But you've been gone for quite a while.

You spoke words that sound the same,
The echo rings with someone else's name,
Does she wonder why you're never still,
Always chasing the next thrill?

Does she know the truth inside,
That you're only here for the ride?
She'll be left to wonder why,
When you change your heart like you change your mind.

But when the night falls, and you're alone,
Do you miss the love you once called home?
Does she see the fragile walls you've made,
Or is she caught in your charade?

How long can you play this game?
Changing faces, but it's all the same,
In your arms, she feels so safe,
But you're just leading her to a darker place.

You've built a house of cards so tall,
But soon it's bound to take a fall,
And when it does, where will you be?
Lost in your own debris?

Do you feel the emptiness,
Hollow where your heart should rest?
Does she know, or does she see,
The man behind the mystery?

Does she know the path you choose
Is paved with souls that you misuse?
I see you now with someone new,
But one day, she'll see it too.

I Only Saw What I Wanted to See

Golden leaves fall, painting the ground,
Speaking of memories without a sound.
In the stillness of the night, I see
Reflections of what used to be.

We danced through the storms, hand in hand,
Built castles of dreams in the sand.
But time has a way of changing plans,
Leaving us where we stand.

Reflections of yesterday,
In the mirrors of our minds,
Shadows that won't fade away,
Echoes of better times.
We were young and we were free,
In a world of make believe,
But the dreams have flown away,
Leaving reflections of yesterday.

We laughed and we cried, heart to heart,
Promised we'd never be apart.
But life has a way of making art
Out of our broken parts.
Now the stars above remind me of
All the shared dreams and love,
In the silence, I hear your voice,
Telling me we had no choice.

I only saw what I wanted to see,
In your eyes, a perfect lie, a fantasy,
Blinded by love, I was so naive,
I only saw what I wanted to see.

Now I see through the lies, I realize,
The truth was always there, in disguise,
Blinded by love, I was so naive,
I only saw what I wanted to see.

We soared high on wings of dreams,
Caught in love's enchanting streams.
But fate has a way of tearing seams,
Unraveling our perfect schemes.

You were my light, or so I believed,
But the glow in your eyes was just what I perceived.
I chased every dream, blinded by fate,
Only to find out, it was all too late.

I only saw what I wanted to see,
Living in a fantasy, just you and me.
But the mirrors don't lie, and the tears finally show,
I was lost in a love that I didn't really know.

Ruins of Us

I gave you my love, you replaced it with hate,
Sacrificing myself for your sake.
Standing at your altar, holding shards of my soul,
Drowning in the waters of the lies you told.

I built up walls to keep out the pain,
But they crumbled at the sound of your name.
Now I'm standing in the ruins of us,
Wondered why I gave you my trust.

Wondering wastelands where we used to be,
Searching for the scattered fragments of me.
This was a place where love once bloomed,
Now all that's left are memories in dusty, old rooms.

You took my light and left me in the dark,
Tore down the dreams I once held in my heart.
You burned our bridges, left nothing behind,
Now I'm lost in these ruins, losing my mind.

I search the sky for a sign of you,
But the stars don't shine the way they used to.
They've dimmed and faded, like the fire we let die,
Leaving only questions of how and why.

In the mirror, I see a stranger's face,
Reflecting this person that's fallen from grace.
Turning away, I can't bear to see
This broken thing you've made of me.
Reaching for a love that no longer exists,
Craving a taste of your poisonous lips,
Caught in a trap of your sweet disguise,
Blinded by the glow of your deceptive eyes.

In dreams, I see your face once more,
But it's not the same as it was before.
It can't cleanse the scars you made,
Or heal the heart that you betrayed.

I used to dream of a life with you,
I tried to find solace in the places we knew,
Searching for answers that never arrived,
Screaming in silence without your replies.

I gave you my love, but now it's all gone,
Since I have nothing left, it's time to move on.
This pain you inflicted won't define who I am,
So I want you to know, I don't give a goddamn.

Broken Thing

I am an ugly broken thing.
Where do I end? Where do I begin?
Bound by guilt, by fear, by sin,
This ugly, dreadful, broken thing.

Cracked is the mirror, so is my soul,
Patchwork pieces that others stole.
I wear these scars, to tell the tale,
Of battles won and battles failed.

Vacant eyes stare back at me,
A hollow shell, where I cease to be,
A tainted soul, doomed to die,
No escape or alibi.

I am a wasted, wretched thing,
A monster I am battling,
Hidden this horrid image I bring,
This wasted, wretched, rotten thing.

There is no joy, there is no peace,
No cure for this consuming disease.
Just this cold and empty space,
Where I drift, lost in this place.

No hope, no dawn, no saving grace,
Just painful memories I can't erase.
This ugly, rotten, broken thing,
Collapsing under fractured wings.

I am a horrid, frightful thing,
This fragile cage is crumbling.
How do I fight this beast within?
This horrid, awful, frightful thing.

Sinking deeper in the void,
Where hope and faith are both destroyed,
This creature, it will not survive,
Barely breathing, barely alive.

Solace does not comfort me through
No roads that lead to something new.
The scars are deep, the wounds still bleed,
No life can grow from this dead seed.

I am a poisoned, dying thing,
A marionette with severed strings,
Wearing the darkness as my skin,
This poisoned, wilted, dying thing.

Tangled in webs that I can't see,
Chains that bind invisibly,
Crawling through this misery,
No path ahead, no destiny.

Falling through endless space,
Where shadows stretch and darkness waits,
A tattered soul with cracks that spread,
Dwelling among the living dead.
I am a crumbled, lonely thing,
A ghost that haunts its own suffering.
The mirror shows me who I've been,
This crooked, crumbled, lonely thing.

A heart that's lost its will to beat,
Out of control and incomplete,
Drowning in the endless black,
Who could love a monster like that?

A broken thing, a scattered mind,
Searching for what I'll never find,
Slipping deep beneath the weight,
Of bitter love and twisted fate.

I am this shattered, fractured thing,
With hollow eyes and crippled wings,
The night consumes, it softly sings,
To take this wretched, mangled thing.

Section III: The Fallout

Heartbreak is not a moment but a mosaic, pieced together with shards of "almosts" and "what ifs," a tapestry woven from the threads of dreams that unraveled long before we dared to let go.

Too Much

I'm too broken,
Too lost,
I'm too fragile,
Too unsure,
I'm too uncertain.
I'm too weak,
I'm too distant,
I'm too impure,

I'm too conflicted,
I'm too torn,
I'm too burdened,
I'm too worn.
I'm too doubtful,
I'm too stressed,
Too anxious and too depressed,
I'm too stubborn,
I'm too afraid,
Too far gone in the mess I made.

I'm too lonely,
I'm too sad,
I'm too calm,
I'm too mad,
I'm too loud,
I'm too lost,
I'm too scared,
I'm too crossed.

I'm too closed,
I'm too guarded,
I'm too unaware,
Too broken hearted,
I'm too late,

I'm too spent,
I'm too worried,
I'm too content.

I'm too timid,
I'm too defensive,
I'm too bitter,
I'm too offensive,
I'm too hurt,
I'm too bruised,
I'm too unprepared,
I'm too confused.

I'm too shy,
I'm too reserved,
I'm too clingy,
I'm too unnerved,
I'm too cautious,
I'm too relaxed,
I'm too angry,
I'm too complex.

Can't and Won't

I can't see the light,
I can't find my way,
I can't hold on,
I can't seize the day,
I can't make a move,
I can't take a stand,
I can't reach out,
I can't lend a hand.

I won't change,
I won't bend,
I won't break,
I won't pretend,
I won't give in,
I won't try,
I won't believe,
I won't deny.

I won't risk,
I won't dare,
Won't open up,
Cause I won't care.
I won't embrace,
I won't reach,
I won't listen,
I won't teach.

I can't be brave,
I can't be strong,
I can't find where I belong,
I can't see hope,
I can't find peace,
I can't feel joy,
I can't find release.

No,
I won't smile,
I won't play,
I won't laugh,
I won't stay,
I won't reach,
I won't give,
I won't move,
I won't live.

I won't forgive,
I won't forget,
I won't find solace,
I won't reset,
I won't mend,
I won't repair,
I won't move on,
I won't disappear.

Call Me Crazy

You called me crazy,
You thought you played me,
But I'm not the one who's lost their mind.
You called me crazy,
You thought you'd break me,
Don't worry baby, I'll be just fine.

You tried to change me,
To rearrange me
Into someone who'd fit your design.
You underestimated,
But now it's faded,
Your control won't hold this heart of mine.

You took for granted
All that was handed
On a silver platter, my love and care.
But now it's over,
I'm getting closer
To a future where you're not there.

You spun your stories,
In all your glory,
But your façade is crumbling down.
You tried to mold me,
But can't control me,
I'm rising up, I won't drown.

In the darkest hour,
You thought your power
Would keep me begging at your door.
But now it's ending,
No more pretending,
I don't need you anymore.

In my reflection,
No more rejection,
Just the strength that you could never see.
I've found my vision,
In my decision,
To live life for only me.

So, call her crazy,
But listen clearly,
You had the world and didn't know,
Crazy for hoping,
Crazy for loving,
But you were crazy for letting her go.

Steppingstones

Was I just your steppingstone,
A place to rest before you roam?
Did you use my love to grow?
Tell me now, I need to know.

I thought we were building something real,
But now it's clear how you feel.
You took my love, left me alone,
I was just your steppingstone.

Every word, every touch,
Was it ever really love?
Now I'm left with empty space,
Trying to forget your face.

I was a fool, I played the part,
Believing you would guard my heart.
Thought we had plans, you had your own,
And I was just your steppingstone.

Counterfeit love, sweet and vile,
A toxic kiss, a deadly smile.
You left me here, a hollow shell,
Trapped within this living hell.

You took my love, you took my trust,
Crushed them both into dust.
I was the bridge you crossed with ease,
A tool to satisfy your needs.
You said forever, but meant goodbye,
Leaving me here to wonder why.
Didn't see the lies behind your eyes,
The hidden plans and alibis.

You saw my light and craved its glow,
Now I'm drowning in your undertow,
My heart was yours; I made it known,
But I was just your steppingstone.

I watched you leave without a trace,
No regret upon your face.
Did you lay in my embrace,
While planning your great escape?

Was I only meant to break,
So that you could rise, for your own sake?
Did you find what you were searching for,
Or did you lose yourself once more?

Do you sleep with an unburdened heart,
Knowing how you tore mine apart?
You climbed so high, left me in defeat,
Was I just the dirt beneath your feet?

All the things we used to say,
Haunts me less each passing day,
So here's to you, my steppingstone,
The love we had, I've now outgrown.

Lethal Love

You were my fatal distraction,
Sweet devastation,
The most exquisite form of self-ruination,
Bliss and dysfunction,
Hearts caught in slow motion,
A splendid and venomous kind of affliction.

You were my reckless fascination,
Pure obliteration,
We danced together on the edge of temptation,
Midnight contradiction,
Heartache dressed in fiction,
A peaceful decent into sinister addictions.

You were my quiet disaster,
Soft-spoken master,
The untamable storm I was chasing after,
Slow-burn obsession,
Symphony of imperfection,
We burned in the flames of our own resurrection.

You were my great surrender,
Last defender,
Tangled in the webs of our own splendor,
Torn and tattered,
Unfinished letters,
A love I never thought would shatter.

You were the break in the silence,
Love soaked in violence,
A heart dressed in calm and defiance,
Mirrored reflections,
Guilty reflection,
Each moment built on subtle deception.

You were my broken redemption,
Flawed creation,
Wrapped in layers of misdirection,
Fading illusion,
A beautiful intrusion,
Blurring the lines between love and delusion.

You were my love in suppression,
An endless procession
Of feelings I hid with careful discretion,
A smothered eruption,
Whispered seduction,
A love that defied all sense and function.

You were my deepest confession,
A bittersweet lesson,
A love too dangerous to be spoken or mentioned,
You were my perfect mistake,
The risk I chose to take,
Even if it meant every part of me would break.

You were my shadowed dimension,
A dream in deflection,
The silent cause of my soul's self-deprecation,
Unending vibration,
A soft disintegration,
We crumble beneath the weight of our realizations.

You were my forsaken pursuit,
A seed that took root,
A love not meant to bare any fruit,
Fragile resistance,
Bound in persistence,
We defied logic with ruthless insistence.

You were my moonlight rapture,
Innocence fractured,
Spinning in a world that we manufactured,
My unfinished war,
The battle that I swore,
To win, but I can't fight anymore.

I Don't Know You

There was a time when I felt for you,
Savored your words like honeydew,
But these stars don't shine like they used to,
I don't know you.

You've become a silhouette
Wrapped so neatly in my regret.
Can't remember, can't forget,
I don't know you.

My tongue has forgotten how,
My body will not allow
Your name to come out of my mouth,
We're just fairytales now.

I held on as you withdrew,
Never thought I would stop caring for you.
You moved on, I can't pursue,
I don't know you.

You walked away, you couldn't see
The emptiness you left in me,
A husk of who I used to be
I don't know you.

I like to pretend I do,
Holding on while slipping from view,
A phase you were going through,
I don't know you.

You can't cleanse the scars you made,
Or heal the heart that you betrayed,
You wanted it to be this way,
I don't know you.

You didn't spare a second glance,
Left me in the aftermath,
Continued in indifference,
I don't know you.

I wanted to believe your lies,
The only truth was your goodbye,
Is he still there behind your eyes?
I don't know you.

Is it fate or just a cruel mistake?
A broken heart that won't quite break.
Maybe hearts learn from what they forsake,
I don't know you.

Years go by and seasons change,
But our paths will never cross again,
Forgotten myth that no one claimed,
I don't know you.

I built my world on the things you said,
But I don't know you like I thought I did.
Every promise rendered invalid,
I don't know you.

The chapter closed before I knew
The person you had turned into,
But stars fall and fade as people often do,
I don't know you.

I'm a stranger, you don't even see,
Gentle apathy, resting in neutrality.
These ghosts of who we used to be,
I don't know you; you don't know me.

Section IV: The Reflection

There is beauty in this becoming, in the quiet alchemy of turning pain into poetry, and loss into light. We look into the mirror, not to see what has been broken, but to find the strength that blooms in the cracks.

More Than This

Within these bones, a madness lies,
A thirst for more than what the world supplies,
To seize the moments, bold and wise,
Drown in life and be reborn.

In obscurity, where secrets hide,
Where dreams and nightmares coincide,
With open arms and heart untied,
I'll wander through the storm.

Unyielding to the world's disguise,
In the echoes of ancient cries,
Through every fall, a soul must rise
To greet the coming dawn.

In echoes of a distant song,
Where memories and hopes both belong,
The pathway ever true and long,
Beneath the rising sun.

Through valleys dark and mountains high,
Beneath the ever-watchful skies,
The spirit soars with courage that defies,
To find where we belong.

In the eyes of those who dared to dream,
Reflecting, a familiar scene,
A river flowing to the stream
Of time that slips away.

The moonlight guides the weary soul
Through uncharted paths and endless roads,
To find the peace that makes us whole,
And journeys on its way.

In gardens where the roses bloom,
Every step dispels the doom,
Casts away all thoughts of gloom,
And starts each day anew.

So let the madness in me rise,
To challenge fate, claim the prize.
With open heart and open eyes,
And cherish every view.

Self-Discovery

The voice in my head is conflicting,
Pulling me apart,
Each shouting a different fate,
Each tugging at my heart.

My mind's a stormy sea,
Waves crashing in my soul,
Tossing me from hope to fear,
Stripping me out of control.

Is there a map to guide me,
Through this labyrinth of doubt?
A light to shine upon my way,
Show me how to get out.

Paths stretching out before me,
Each with its own allure,
Promises of fulfillment,
Yet none of them feel sure.

The fear of choosing wrong,
It paralyzes me.
What if the path I pick
Is not my destiny?

I don't know what I want,
I'm lost, wandering blind.
It's haunting, taunting me
So many choices in my mind.

I'm caught in indecision,
A maze without a guide.
Every option tempting,
Yet none fits inside.

Will I find my purpose,
Amidst the shifting sands?
Can I break free from this web
Spun by my own hands?

Dreams that once seemed vivid,
Now blur and fade away,
Leaving me in darkness,
I'm afraid I'll lose my way.

I question every motive,
I doubt each planned design,
Seeking a clear answer,
A single, solid sign.

Amidst the fog of thoughts,
I search for inner peace,
A place where I can anchor,
And let my worries cease.

In the tangled maze of self,
Daunting it may be
I'll find my path and journey on
In the discovery of me.

Graffiti

The walls of my heart are adorned in graffiti,
Colors and words, a chaotic city.
Each stroke a memory, each line a scar,
Narratives of battles, of who you are.

Bright hues of joy, somber shades of pain,
Moments of sunshine, torrents of rain.
Names etched in passion, crossed out in grief,
Layers of history—built belief by belief.

There are messages of hope, penned in haste,
Dreams that were chased and then laid to waste.
Promises broken, vows that were kept,
Tears that were hidden, nights that you forget.

Sketches of laughter, outlines of sorrow,
Visions of yesterday, fears of tomorrow.
A mural of feelings, a canvas of thought,
Lessons from battles, both lost and fought.

In corners, you'll find secrets concealed,
Truths hidden and lies revealed.
Fragments and echoes of screams,
Tangled in the web of forgotten dreams.

The walls of my soul are a tapestry woven,
With threads of my life, both given and stolen.
A gallery open, for all who might see,
The beautiful chaos that defines me.

Burning and Clearing

I took a step into the unknown,
Left behind the things I've outgrown.
The weight of silence in the air,
Can't tell if freedom or despair.

Maybe both paths lead to change,
What we lose and what we gain.
Am I breaking away or learning to heal?
Am I burning a bridge or clearing the field?

Every choice feels like a spark,
Am I igniting or tearing apart?
Standing here where the smoke won't clear,
I'm caught between hope and fear.

Only time will let me know,
Which way this story's gonna go.
But here I stand, heart unsealed,
Am I burning a bridge or clearing the field?

The road behind me fades away,
But I still hear the words we didn't say.
Are we meant to crash or fly,
Or let the past just pass us by?

Caught in the middle between right and wrong,
Don't know if I'm weak or if I'm strong.
If I let go, will the truth be revealed?
Am I burning a bridge or clearing the field?
Maybe the fire's what I need,
To finally plant a brand-new seed.
The ashes falling like the rain,
Could wash away the scars and pain.

Every flame has its cost,
But every line that's crossed is not always lost.
I'm chasing something, but is it real?
Am I burning a bridge or clearing the field?

I'm standing here with matches in my hand,
At the edge of everything we planned,
The sky is on fire, but I can't tell
If it's freedom rising or a farewell.

Standing on the edge, I look back at the flame,
Don't know if I'm proud or if I'm ashamed.
If I walk away, will the wounds be sealed?
Am I burning a bridge or clearing the field?

Maybe it's time to let it burn,
To find the strength I never learned.
For every tear that falls in vain,
I'll plant a seed inside the flame.

I wonder if you feel it too,
The weight of all that we've been through,
To all the fears I've concealed—
Am I burning a bridge or clearing the field?

I stand between the dusk and dawn,
Wondering where I belong.
Do I hold the flame, or let it die?
Do I trust the truth or live the lie?
I don't know if it's a fable or fate,
A little too soon or a little too late.
On this path, I've got no shield,
Maybe I'm both burning the bridge and clearing the field.

Made in Mistakes

I was made in mistakes,
built from the breaks,
Found in the moments
that I thought were too late.
Every fall, every bruise,
every road I didn't choose
Led me to this place,
I was made in mistakes.

I've made peace with my past,
With all my wrongs,
Turned the pain into purpose,
And silence to poems.
The hurt and the healing,
They both have a place
In the story I'm telling,
I was made in mistakes.

I've wrestled with questions
That had no reply,
But the answers I needed
Were in the goodbye.
Each closed door behind me,
Taught me to embrace
That what's gone was a lesson,
I was made in mistakes.

I was stitched by the storms
through chaos reborn.
Every tear, every scar,
shaped the path that I am on.
All of the detours and every delay,
Was carving the road
That led me this way.

I've learned how to break
Without breaking apart,
How to carry the weight
Of a fragmented heart.
I've found my own rhythm
In the beats that I missed,
In the moments of quiet
Where bliss can exist.

I was made in mistakes,
Crafted from pain,
Every misstep apart of the change.
The pieces that shattered,
Still found their grace,
In the life I'm rebuilding,
I was made in mistakes.

Now every fail is a footnote
In the journey I've walked,
Every regret just a chapter,
In the lessons I've sought.
I see beauty in breaking,
And strength in the ache,
I was never forsaken,
I was made in mistakes.
I've danced with the darkness,
Felt lost in the storm,
But it's there I discovered
What my heart was made for.
The fears that I buried, the devils I've faced,
became part of me,
I was made in mistakes.

Every tear I was shedding
Was watering the ground,
Of a life still becoming,
Of a self newly found.

For a future that's certain,
For a soul that won't shake,
I'm not just surviving,
I'm made in mistakes.

Each scar is a chapter,
Of strength born from strain,
Every stumble a step
Towards what I became.
And though I was broken,
I've learned to embrace,
That beauty is woven
Through every mistake.

Growing Up

Who will I be when I grow up?
Will I get it together or still screw it up?
Still tripping over love and luck,
I'm getting older but I'm not growing up.

They said time would teach me all I need to know,
But the lessons fade while doubts still grow.
I thought the years would wipe the slate so clean,
But the same old ghosts haunt every scene.

They say, "settle down, find something real,"
But what's more real than the way I feel?
They shake their heads, say it's just a phase,
But I've been like this for all my days.

I keep wondering if I've wasted my time,
Chasing illusions that cost me my mind,
I build my hopes up like castles of sand,
Trying to follow life's shifting demands.

Is there a purpose? A reason to be?
Where is the pathway that's hidden from me?
I'm traveling down roads that lead to nowhere,
Feeling the weight of every unanswered prayer.

I'm reaching for dreams that are out of my touch,
Pouring my heart into bottomless cups,
Chasing shadows, but it's never enough,
I'm getting older, but I'm not growing up.
The years go by, but I stay the same,
Searching for the girl with my name.
I wonder if I'll ever change
Or if I'm meant to stay this way.

I've been running in circles, chasing my doubt,
Still trying to figure out what life's all about.
Will I make sense of the life I've begun?
Who will I be when this journey is done?

Is there a moment where it all makes sense?
A reason behind the consequence?
They say wisdom comes with the price of years,
But I've bought mine with blood and tears.

They tell me slow down, take it easy,
But living too careful never pleased me,
I'll fall and rise a thousand more,
That's what this heart of mine is for.

Here's to the stumbles and to the scars,
The broken roads that made us who we are,
I'll run wild, even if I fall,
Growing up doesn't mean growing small.

Conclusion

The Salt We Bleed has been a journey through the many shades of the human heart—its capacity to love deeply, to break, to mend, and to begin again. This collection is a journey through the most intimate corners of the human heart, reflecting the joys, sorrows, and complexities that define our lives.

It is a path marked by the echoes of love that once filled our hearts, the pain that lingers long after, and the quiet strength that rises from the rubble of all we've lost. Each poem was crafted to resonate with the universal experiences of love, heartbreak, and the ongoing quest for identity.

The poems within *The Salt We Bleed* are meant to be a mirror, reflecting the universal experiences that bind us all. Whether you have found yourself in the euphoria of new love, the pain of unraveling, the desolation of heartbreak, or the quiet peace of self-reflection. The salt we bleed, the tears we shed, and the scars we bear are not signs of weakness, but of survival. They are the proof that we have lived, that we have loved, and that we have dared to feel every facet of our humanity.

The journey of life is a series of moments—some filled with light and others shrouded in darkness. It is in navigating these moments that we find our true selves and build our unique stories. This collection has taken us through the blossoming of love, its inevitable unraveling, the fallout that follows, and the reflection that ultimately leads us back to ourselves.

Thank you for allowing *The Salt We Bleed* to be a part of your path, and may you continue to walk forward with courage, with hope, and with the knowledge that you are always worthy of the love and light that await you. May these poems continue to play in your heart and mind, offering solace, inspiration, and a deeper connection to your own experiences.

Acknowledgments

The creation of *The Salt We Bleed* has been a journey of vulnerability, discovery, and unearthing truths that often lay hidden beneath the surface. It is a collection shaped not just by my own experiences but by the unwavering support, guidance, and inspiration of so many incredible souls who walked beside me, each leaving their mark on these pages.

To my husband—your love has been the foundation upon which this journey was built. Thank you for being my unwavering believer, and my constant source of strength. Your endless encouragement has been the thread that held me together, especially during the moments when I doubted my voice, my words, and my worth. You have taught me what it means to love unconditionally.

To every reader who holds this collection in their hands—thank you. You are the final, most essential part of this journey. It is your willingness to listen, to feel, and to find pieces of your own story within these poems that gives them life. Without you, these words would be nothing more than ink on a page.

To my friends, family and confidants, who have been the keepers of my secrets, the ones who listened to countless drafts, and the voices that offered encouragement when the road seemed long, and the destination unclear—I am endlessly grateful. You stood by me through sleepless nights, creative blocks, and moments of vulnerability, offering not just your support but your truth, pushing me to dig deeper and to be bolder in my storytelling. You are the quiet strength behind these words, the laughter that softened the hard days, and the light that guided me back to myself.

Lastly, to the moments of heartbreak, love, loss, and growth that inspired this work—thank you. It is through you that I learned to find my voice, to embrace the beauty of my scars, and to understand that every wound carries within it the seed of something beautiful.

You are the salt that runs through these pages, the essence that binds this journey together.

The Salt We Bleed would not exist without the countless hands, hearts, and voices that have touched my life, and it is with immense gratitude and humility that I offer this collection to you. Thank you for walking this path with me, for believing in the power of words, and for reminding me that we are never truly alone in our stories.

Author's Bio

Denile Baugh is a poet, writer, and explorer of the human experience, born and raised in Kingston, Jamaica. Denile discovered her passion for poetry at a young age, finding solace and expression in the rhythm of language and the power of storytelling. It was in the bustling streets and vibrant culture of her hometown that she first began to understand the power of words—to heal, to connect, and to transform.

Denile's journey as a writer began in earnest when she joined the Jamaica Youth Theatre, where she not only honed her craft but also developed a deep appreciation for the performing arts. This experience allowed her to blend her love for language with the rhythm and cadence of spoken word, earning her bronze, silver, and gold medals in the Jamaica Cultural Development Commission (JCDC) Annual Poetry Competition in 2005, 2007, and 2009, respectively. These early achievements marked the beginning of a lifelong commitment to exploring the nuances of human emotion and the delicate balance between joy and sorrow, love and loss.

Over the years, Denile's work has evolved into a heartfelt exploration of themes such as love, heartbreak, identity, and resilience. Her writing is characterized by its raw honesty, vivid imagery, and melodic flow, drawing inspiration from her own experiences as well as the shared human condition. She believes that poetry is more than just words on a page—it is a summons to feel, to question, and to connect with the world around us and the world within ourselves.

The Salt We Bleed, Denile's debut chapbook, is a culmination of years spent navigating the complexities of love, loss, and self-discovery. It is a deeply personal collection that speaks to the universal experience of what it means to be human—to be vulnerable, to be broken, and to find the strength to rise again. With each poem, she invites readers to step into the intimate spaces of their own hearts, to explore the salt and sweetness of life, and to embrace the beauty that can be found in even the most painful moments.

Denile draws inspiration from a diverse range of influences, from the rich oral traditions of her Jamaican heritage to the works of contemporary poets and lyricists who have shaped her understanding of storytelling. Her writing is infused with a deep sense of rhythm, echoing the sounds and stories of her childhood, and carries with it a sense of longing, hope, and resilience that speaks to readers from all walks of life.

Now residing in Hartford, Connecticut, Denile continues to explore the many facets of human experiences through her poetry, using her voice to shed light on the themes that connect us all. She is committed to the belief that words have the power to heal, to challenge, and to inspire, and she strives to create work that resonates with authenticity, compassion, and truth. Denile remains dedicated to her craft, to the art of vulnerability, and to the belief that every story, no matter how small, is worth telling.

www.ingramcontent.com/pod-product-compliance
Lightning Source LLC
LaVergne TN
LVHW050939080826
845145LV00004B/1332

* 9 7 8 1 9 6 6 3 6 9 5 7 8 *